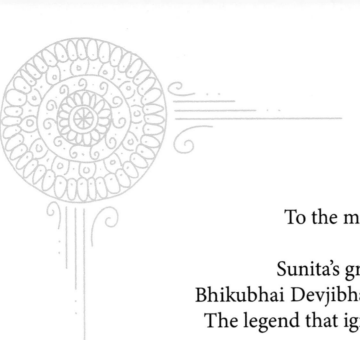

To the memory of

Sunita's grandfather
Bhikubhai Devjibhai Lad (1918-2020).
The legend that ignited my curiosity.

Acknowledgement

Dear Sagarbhai Shukla, Hindu Priest.
Thank you for passing your knowledge
and wisdom onto the next generation.

Published by The Jai Jais Ltd
Copyright Sunita Shah and James Ballance
All rights reserved
The Jai Jais is a Registered Trademark of The Jai Jais Ltd
The moral right of the authors and illustrator has been asserted
ISBN 978-1-9163242-1-3

The Jai Jais®
Legends Series

The Hanuman Chalisa
For Children

by Sunita Shah, Malvi Raval, and Rishi Handa

Illustrated by James Ballance

Contents

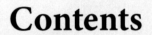

Who is Hanuman?

Lord Hanuman is known as the 'Monkey God', and commander of the monkey (vanara) army. His name originates from the Sanskrit 'hanu' meaning "jaw", and 'man' meaning "prominent" or "disfigured". Ancient history claimed he received his name during childhood when Indra, king of the gods, struck him in the jaw for attempting to leap up and grab the sun.

It is said that Hanuman is the incarnation of Lord Shiva, and he is known as the divine devotee of Lord Rama. Hanuman is one of the central characters of the Hindu epic Ramayana.

What is the Hanuman Chalisa?

The Hanuman Chalisa is a Hindu devotional prayer addressed to Lord Hanuman. It was written long ago in the sixteenth-century, by the poet Tulsidas. He was imprisoned by the Mughal Empero Aurangzeb. The emperor had mocked Tulsidas, who was well known for his devotion to Lord Rama. The emperor challenged Tulsidas to show him Lord Rama. The poet cleverly replied that seeing Lord Rama was not possible without true devotion. The emperor was angered and Tulsidas was imprisoned. He was in prison when he wrote the Chalisa.

Hanuman Chalisa holds a special place and importance in the Hindu tradition as it reveals Hanuman's many qualities such as strength, courage and wisdom. The word 'chalisa' means "forty"; the Hanuman Chalisa has forty verses.

3.

Why do people recite it?

Hindus believe that reciting the Chalisa will bring Hanuman to their help in challenging times. This amazing monkey god will help to ward off evil spirits and negative energy. Each verse of the Chalisa has its own significance.

The main day that is dedicated to Hanuman is Saturday; devotees also dedicate Tuesday to his worship. Hanuman's favourite offerings are flowers, jasmine oil, and sindoor (vermillion-orange powder). He loves sweet offerings made from jaggery (raw sugar), and nuts. Saffron is his favorite colour!

What are the benefits?

Warding off evil spirits is one of the most powerful results of reciting the Chalisa. Hanuman is a god who banishes evil and harmful spirits. The Chalisa will also help get rid of scary and fearful thoughts, which is why young children worship Hanuman.

Everyone makes mistakes, knowingly and unknowingly, but people can ask for forgiveness by reciting the Chalisa. This can bring Hanuman's divine protection and can help to remove and overcome obstacles. It also helps to remove any arguments and misunderstandings that can lead you to feel sad.

Recital of the Chalisa creates positive energies and vibrations. Children who recite the Chalisa will be filled with wisdom and strength. Hanuman really is a very strong god! The Chalisa can help children feel extremely lively and energetic throughout the day, and be filled with happy thoughts.

Sometimes children try to do things that can be challenging or tricky, and can cause them to become sad or frustrated. Turning to Hanuman can help children accomplish difficult tasks. He can bring peace and happiness to our mind, and achieve good health.

A common greeting to welcome Hanuman is, "Jai Bajarangbali".

The language of the Hanuman Chalisa

The Hanuman Chalisa is written in the Avadhi language, a form of medieval Hindi spoken in northern India. It is mainly spoken in the Avadh region of Uttar Pradesh. The name Avadh is associated with Ayodhya, the birthplace of Lord Rama.

In the late medieval period of north Indian history, Avadhi was one of the languages used to convey devotional (bhakti) poetry. The most significant literature in Avadhi was also written by Tulsidas and is called the Ram-charit-manas, also known as the 'Tulsi[das] Ramayana' or 'Hindi Ramayana'.

The original text of the Hanuman Chalisa here may slightly differ from other versions that readers have seen or are used to. This is not to be unexpected as there is no single standard Hanuman Chalisa that publishers use.

9.

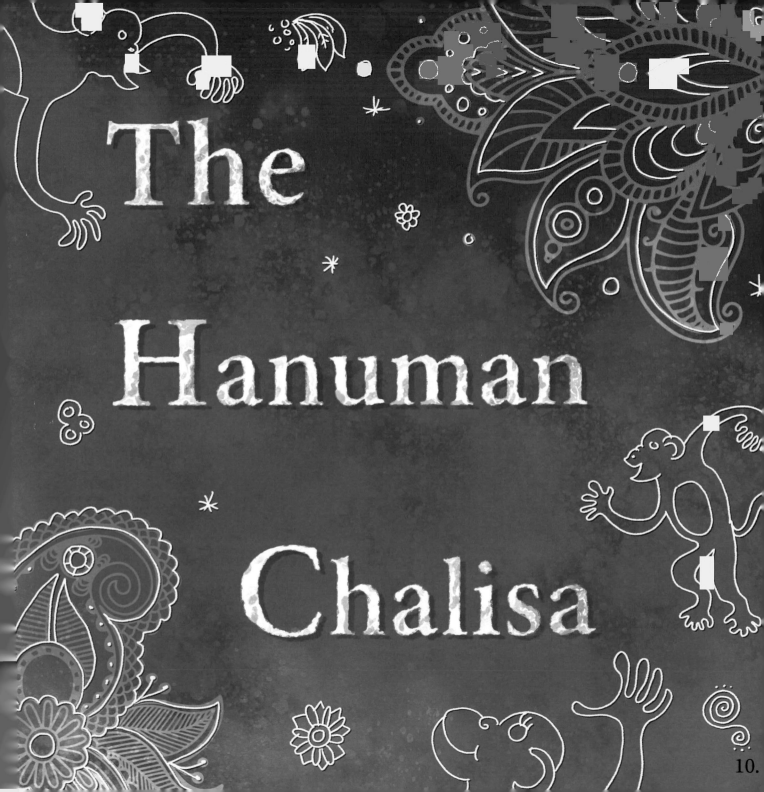

The Hanuman Chalisa

Shree Guru Charana Saroja Raja Nija Manu Mukuru Sudhaari,
Baranau Raghubara Bimala Jasu Jo Daayaku Phala Chaari.

With the dust of Guru's Lotus feet, I first clean the mirror of my heart and then narrate the sacred glory of Shri Rama Chandra, supreme among the Raghu dynasty and the giver of the fourfold attainments of life. These are: dharma, artha, kaama, and moksha (righteous duty, wealth, desire and liberation).

11.

Buddhi-heena Tanu Janike Sumirau Pavana-kumara,
Bala Budhi Vidyaa Dehu Mohi Harahu Kalesa Vikaara.

Knowing myself not to be wise, I request Hanuman, the son of
Pavana, the wind god, to give me strength, intellect and knowledge,
and take away all my miseries and sadness.

Jaya Hanumaana Gyaan Guna Saagara,
Jaya Kapeesa Tihu Loka Ujaagara.

Victory to you, O Hanuman, ocean of wisdom and virtue.
Victory to the lord of the monkeys who is well known in all
three worlds.

Raama Doota Atulita Bala Dhaamaa,
Anjani Putra Pavana-suta Naamaa.

You are the divine messenger of Rama and possessor of
immeasurable strength. You are also known as Anjani-putra
(son of Anjani) and Pavana-putra (son of the wind god).

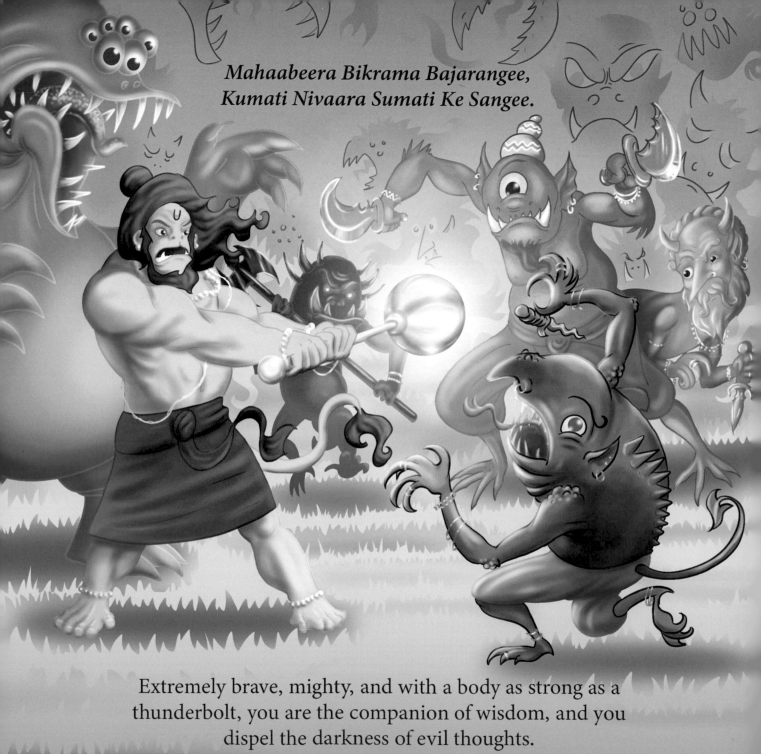

Mahaabeera Bikrama Bajarangee,
Kumati Nivaara Sumati Ke Sangee.

Extremely brave, mighty, and with a body as strong as a
thunderbolt, you are the companion of wisdom, and you
dispel the darkness of evil thoughts.

15.

Kanchana Barana Biraaja Subesaa,
Kaanana Kundala Kunchita Kesaa.

You are golden-coloured and
wear beautiful clothes; you
look beautiful with earrings
and curly hair.

Haatha Bajra Aur Dhvajaa Biraaje,
Kaandhe Moonj Janeoo Saaje.

A thunderbolt and a flag in
your hands, you wear a
sacred thread of moonj
grass on your shoulder.

16.

Shankara Suvana Kesaree-nandana,
Teja Prataapa Mahaa Jaga-bandana.

Vidyaavaan Gunee Ati Chaatura,
Raama Kaaja Karibe Ko Aatura.

Incarnation of Lord Shankara (Lord Shiva), and the pride of Kesari (Hanuman's father), your brilliance and glory are praised by the universe.

The master of knowledge, full of virtue and wisdom, you are always eager to serve Lord Rama.

Prabhu Charitra Sunibe Ko Rasiyaa,
Rama Lakhana Sitaa Mana Basiyaa.

Always keen to listen to Lord Rama's qualities,
you always dwell in the hearts of Shri Rama, Lakshmana and Sita.

18.

Sukshma Roopa Dhari Siyahi Dikhaavaa,
Bikata Roopa Dhari Lanka Jaraavaa.

While you appeared in your humble form to mother Sita, you then
transformed into an awesome size and burnt the city of Lanka.

Bheema Roopa Dhari Asura Sanghaare,
Ramachandra Ke Kaaja Savaare.

With overwhelming might you destroyed
the asuras (demons) and fulfilled Lord Rama's mission.

Laaya Sajeevana Lakhana Jiyaaye,
Shree Raghubeera Harashi Ura Laaye.

You brought the Sanjivani healing herb and restored
Lakshmana back to life. Shri Raghuvira (Shri Rama)
cheerfully embraced you with his heart full of joy.

21.

Raghupati Keenhee Bahuta Badaaee,
Tuma Mama Priya Bharat-hi Sama Bhaaee.

Shri Rama Chandra said you were as dear to him as his own
brother Bharata and praised you highly.

Sahasa Badana Tumharo Jasa Gaavai,
Asa Kahi Shreepati Kantha Lagaavai.

Thousands of living beings are singing your glories,
and Lord Rama took you in his embrace.

Sanakaadika Brahmaadi Muneesaa,
Naarada Saarada Sahita Aheesaa.

Sanaka and his brothers, Lord Brahma (the creator) and the
great sages like Narada, Sarasvati (goddess of learning)
and the serpent Shesha.

24.

Jama Kubera Digapaala Jahaan Te,
Kavi Kovid Kahi Sake Kahaan Te.

Yama (god of death), Kubera (god of wealth), and Digapaala (deputies guarding the four corners of the universe) are unable to express your excellence, then how can poets and scholars do so?

25.

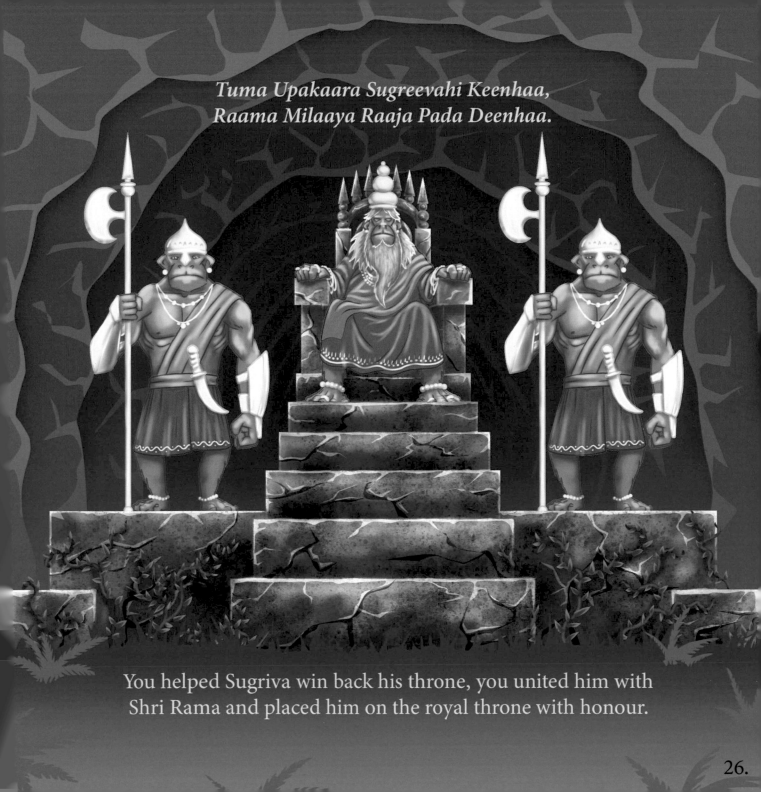

Tuma Upakaara Sugreevahi Keenhaa,
Raama Milaaya Raaja Pada Deenhaa.

You helped Sugriva win back his throne, you united him with
Shri Rama and placed him on the royal throne with honour.

Tumharo Mantra Vibheeshana Maanaa,
Lankeshvara Bhaye Saba Jaga Jaanaa.

By following your advice, Vibhishana became the Lord of Lanka.
This is known all over the universe.

Juga Sahasra Jojana Para Bhaanoo,
Leelyo Taahi Madhura Phala Jaanoo.

You flew to the Sun, which is a fabulous distance of
thousands of miles away, thinking it to be a sweet fruit.

Prabhu Mudrikaa Meli Mukha Maahee,
Jaladhi Laanghi Gaye Acharaja Naahee.

Durgama Kaaja Jagata Ke Jete,
Sugama Anugraha Tumhare Tete.

Keeping the Lord's ring in your mouth,
you easily leapt across the mighty ocean.

With your grace, all the burdens
and difficulties in the world can
be easily overcome

28.

Raama Duaare Tuma Rakhavaare,
Hota Na Aagyaa Binu Paisaare.

You are the keeper of Rama's abode;
no one can enter without your permission.

Saba Sukha Lahai Tumhaaree Saranaa,
Tuma Rakshaka Kaahoo Ko Daranaa.

All comforts of the world are obtained
under your refuge. Devotees can enjoy
divine pleasures and feel fearless under
your protection.

Aapana Teja Samhaaro Aapai,
Teenon Loka Haanka Te Kaampai.

The entire universe trembles at your thunderous
call, and only you can control your own might.

Bhoot Pishaacha Nikata Nahi Aavai,
Mahaabeer Jaba Naama Sunaavai.

No ghosts or spirits can come near when
the name of Lord Hanuman is taken.

Naasai Roga Harai Saba Peeraa,
Japata Nirantara Hanumata Beeraa.

All diseases are destroyed and pain and suffering
are removed when chanting your name regularly,
O brave Hanuman.

Sankata Te Hanumaana Chudaavai,
Mana Krama Bachana Dhyaana Jo Laavai.

Those who remember Hanuman in thought,
word and deed are rescued from troubles in life.

Saba Para Raama Tapasvee Raajaa,
Tina Ke Kaaja Sakala Tuma Saajaa.

You accomplished all the missions of the
hermit King Rama, the ruler of all.

34.

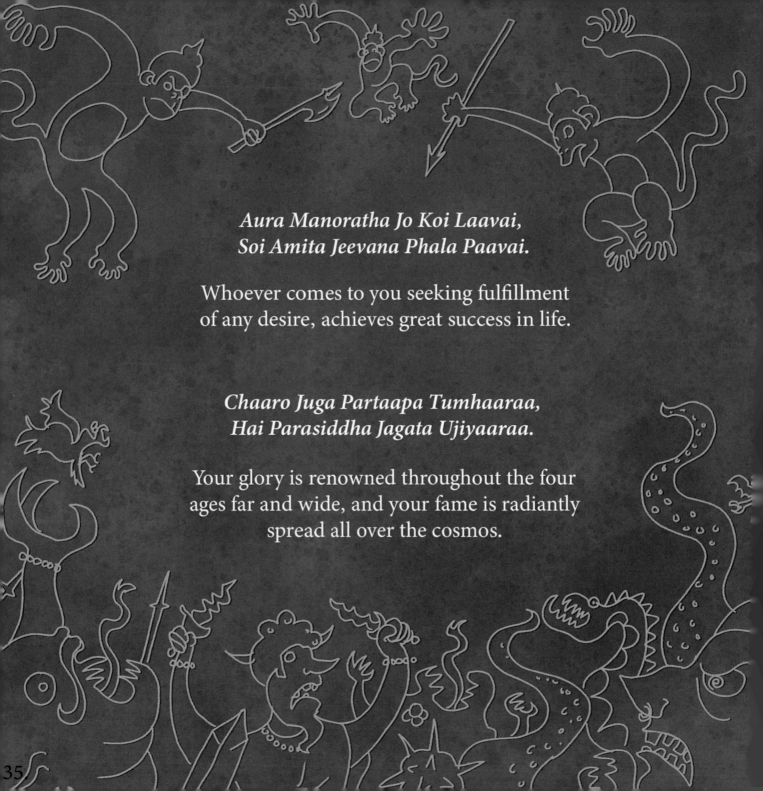

Aura Manoratha Jo Koi Laavai,
Soi Amita Jeevana Phala Paavai.

Whoever comes to you seeking fulfillment
of any desire, achieves great success in life.

Chaaro Juga Partaapa Tumhaaraa,
Hai Parasiddha Jagata Ujiyaaraa.

Your glory is renowned throughout the four
ages far and wide, and your fame is radiantly
spread all over the cosmos.

The guardian and protector of saints and sages, you are the remover
of evil spirits, and demons. Shri Rama has great affection for you.

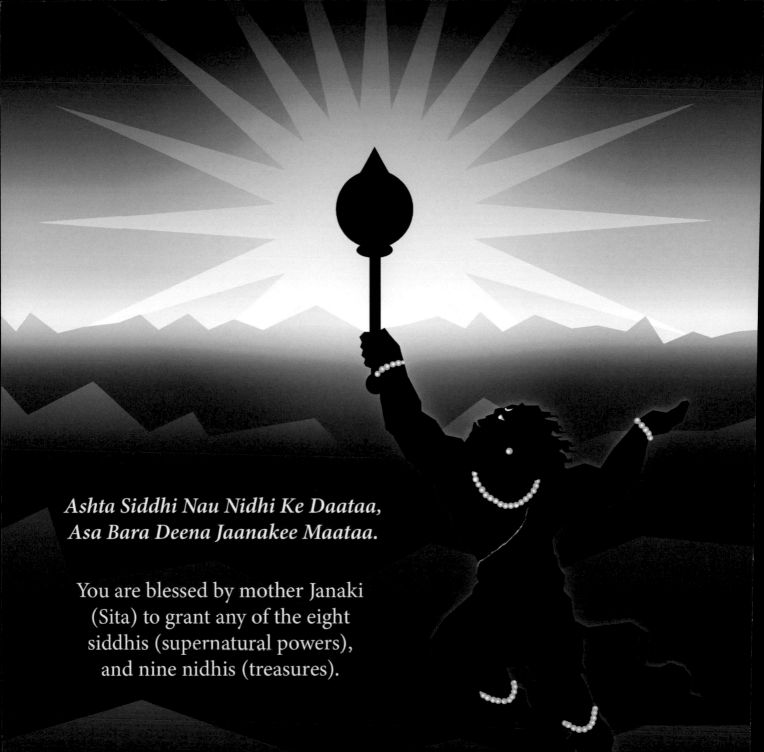

Ashta Siddhi Nau Nidhi Ke Daataa,
Asa Bara Deena Jaanakee Maataa.

You are blessed by mother Janaki
(Sita) to grant any of the eight
siddhis (supernatural powers),
and nine nidhis (treasures).

8 Siddhis (Supernatural powers)
1. Animā: Ability to reduce one's size
2. Mahima: Ability to increase one's size
3. Garima: Ability to increase one's weight infinitely
4. Laghima: Ability to become lighter than the lightest
5. Prāpti: Ability to Obtain anything
6. Prākāmya: Ability to acquire anything desired
7. Isitva: Lordship over creation
8. Vaśitva: Having control over things

9 Nidhis (treasures)
1. Mahapadma: Great lotus flower
2. Padma: Lotus/ a Himalayan lake with treasures
3. Shankha: Conch shell
4. Makara: Crocodile/ Antimony
5. Kachchhapa: Tortoise or turtle shell
6. Mukunda: Cinnabar/ Quick Silver
7. Kunda: Jasmine/ Arsenic
8. Nila: Sapphire/ Antimony
9.Kharva: Cups, vessels baked in fire

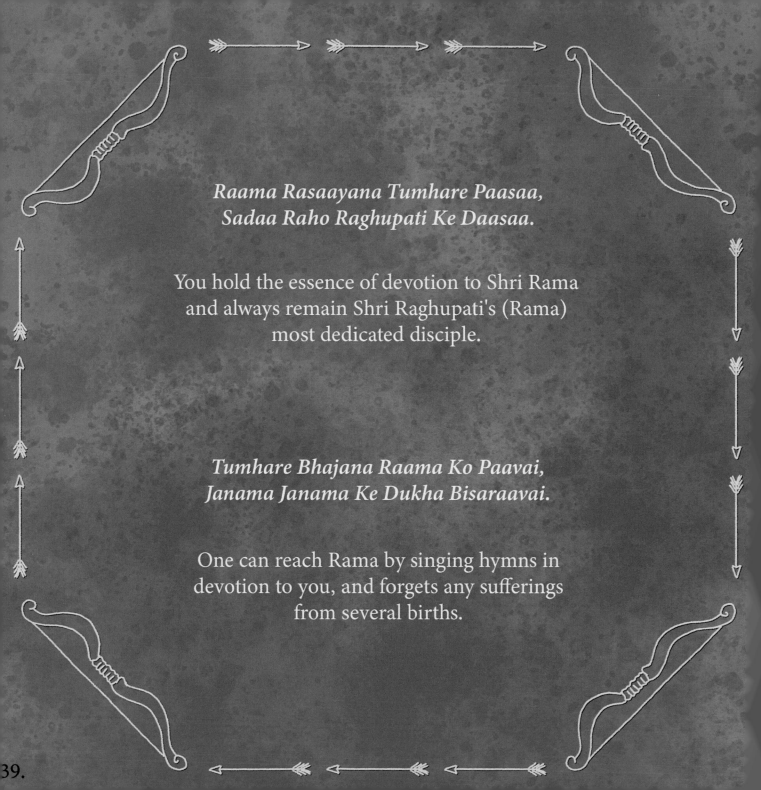

Raama Rasaayana Tumhare Paasaa,
Sadaa Raho Raghupati Ke Daasaa.

You hold the essence of devotion to Shri Rama
and always remain Shri Raghupati's (Rama)
most dedicated disciple.

Tumhare Bhajana Raama Ko Paavai,
Janama Janama Ke Dukha Bisaraavai.

One can reach Rama by singing hymns in
devotion to you, and forgets any sufferings
from several births.

40.

Anta Kaala Raghubara Pura Jaaee,
Jahaa Janma Hari-Bhakta Kahaaee.

At the time of death, one enters the eternal
abode of Shri Rama. Thereafter he'll be born
as a devotee of Shri Rama.

Aura Devataa Chitta Na Dharaee,
Hanumata Se-i Sarba Sukha Karaee.

Even without one's mind on any other deity,
Hanuman alone can give every happiness.

42.

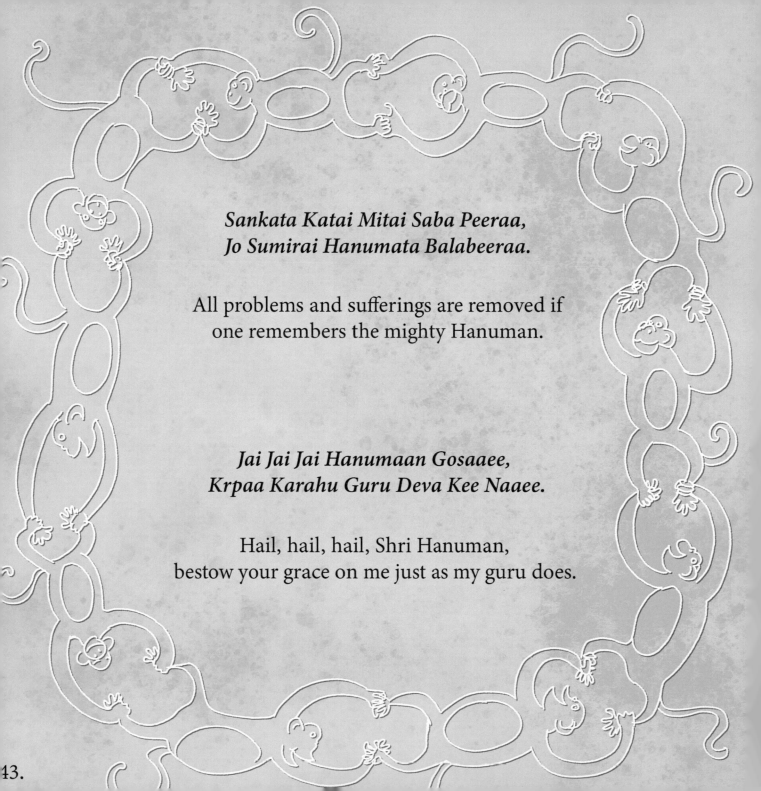

Sankata Katai Mitai Saba Peeraa,
Jo Sumirai Hanumata Balabeeraa.

All problems and sufferings are removed if
one remembers the mighty Hanuman.

Jai Jai Jai Hanumaan Gosaaee,
Krpaa Karahu Guru Deva Kee Naaee.

Hail, hail, hail, Shri Hanuman,
bestow your grace on me just as my guru does.

43.

Jo Sata Baar Paatha Kara Koee,
Chhootahi Bandi Mahaa Sukha Hoee.

He who recite this prayer a hundred times
is free from earthly ties and enjoys the
highest happiness.

Jo Yaha Padhai Hanumaana Chaaleesaa,
Hoya Siddha Saakhee Gaureesaa.

All those who recite this Hanuman Chalisa
attain perfection, as witnessed by Lord Shiva.

47.

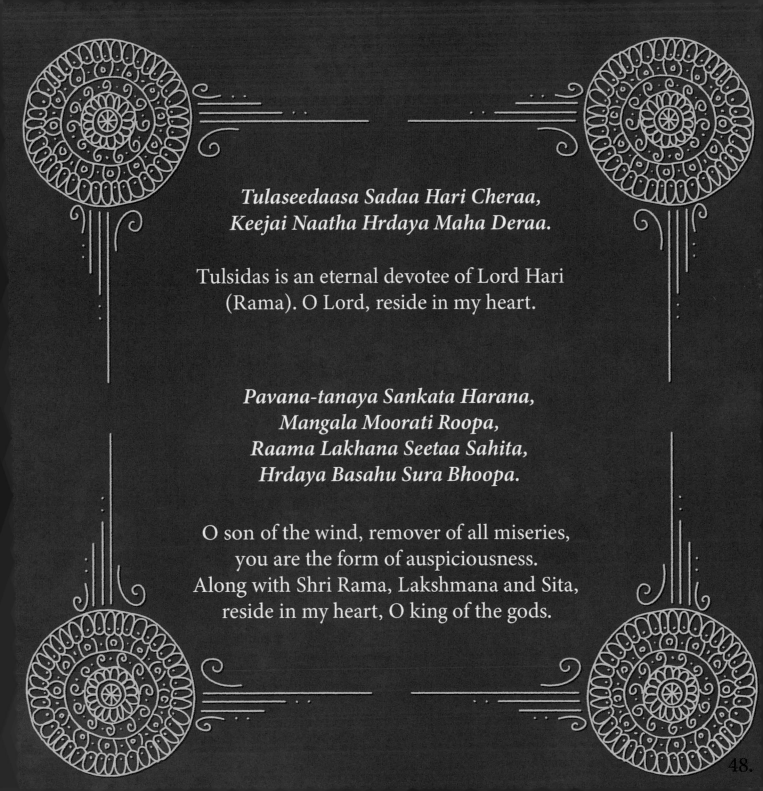

Tulaseedaasa Sadaa Hari Cheraa,
Keejai Naatha Hrdaya Maha Deraa.

Tulsidas is an eternal devotee of Lord Hari
(Rama). O Lord, reside in my heart.

Pavana-tanaya Sankata Harana,
Mangala Moorati Roopa,
Raama Lakhana Seetaa Sahita,
Hrdaya Basahu Sura Bhoopa.

O son of the wind, remover of all miseries,
you are the form of auspiciousness.
Along with Shri Rama, Lakshmana and Sita,
reside in my heart, O king of the gods.

49.

the end.

About the Authors and Illustrator

Sunita Shah BSc (Hons)

Sunita is the mother of two boys, and the creator of, "The Jai Jais" series, which was established in 2015. Her boys inspired her to develop The Jai Jais. She wanted the next generation to connect with their religious and cultural heritage in a modern and engaging way.

Sunita has been a practising speech and language therapist for over 20 years. She has worked as a clinical lead in a senior role within the NHS for 20 years. Sunita now works independently with her private practice "Together Let's Communicate", which has been established for 15 years www.tlc-speechtherapy.co.uk.

Rishi Handa BSc (Hons) PGCE MA PhD

Having been a teacher of maths for many years, Rishi currently teaches Sanskrit as well as philosophy of religion and ethics, and classical Greek at an independent school.

Outside of teaching, he is a professional musician, regularly performing on stage and producing in the studio. He also volunteers as a mentor for an authorship programme which helps train young adults to become skilled writers.

Malvi Raval

Malvi Raval is a Qualified Nurse and co-owner of Poojan Samagri. Malvi is a young entrepreneur that lives in Leicester with her husband and three children. Been brought up in a practising Brahmin household, she has learned from a young age various aspect of the Hindu dharma and their requirements for different poojas.

Over the past 6 years, she has been teaching Hinduism and its values to the younger generation. She is also passionate about keeping the traditions alive and accessible up with scientific rational.

Her passion and energy to help people as a nurse has also been channelled through her entrepreneur spirit when she saw the gap in the market and created Poojan Samagri. Through Poojan Samagri, Malvi is trying to ensure that the next generation have the opportunity to understand the what, why and how of the Hindu rituals and also make it easier for them to acquire the required items.

James Ballance, BA (Hons) Illustration with Animation, UWE

James has worked on various projects including animation, computer games, advertising, and children's books. After moving from Devon to London he worked in a special needs school where he was lucky enough to make the connection with Sunita through staff (thank you Dan!) of the Speech and Language department. www.jamesballance.myportfolio.com

Other products available in The Jai Jais range...

The Jai Jais App
Free download available on iOS and Android.
Includes calendar, flash cards of gods and goddesses, and Ebooks.

Baby Board Books
0-2 years
Shiva
Krishna
Lakshmi
Durga
Hanuman
Ganesh

Main Series
2-4 years
Shiva
Krishna
Lakshmi
Durga
Hanuman
Ganesh
Rama
Saraswati
Kali Ma

Festival Series
4-6 years
Diwali
Holi
Mahavir

Legends Series
6+
Ramayana
Hanuman Chalisa For Children

*Ages are recommendations only.

Head to our website or follow us on social media for more details.

www.thejaijais.com